1 MONTH OF
FREE
READING

at

www.ForgottenBooks.com

By purchasing this book you are eligible for one month membership to ForgottenBooks.com, giving you unlimited access to our entire collection of over 1,000,000 titles via our web site and mobile apps.

To claim your free month visit:

www.forgottenbooks.com/free423655

ISBN 978-0-483-93767-3
PIBN 10423655

THE

PRIVATE LIFE

OF

OHN C. CALHOUN.

A LETTER ORIGINALLY ADDRESSED TO A BROTHER AT THE NORTH,
COMMUNICATED TO THE "INTERNATIONAL MAGAZINE,"
AND NOW REPRINTED AT THE REQUEST OF
MANY PERSONAL FRIENDS.

BY

MISS MARY BATES.

CHARLESTON:
WALKER, RICHARDS AND CO.
MDCCCLII

THE PRIVATE LIFE OF JOHN C. CALHOUN.

———

THE funeral rites of the lamented Calhoun have been performed. So deeply has the mournful pageant impressed me, so vividly have memories of the past been recalled, that I am incapable of thinking or writing upon any other theme. My heart prompts me to garner up my recollections of this illustrious statesman. I can better preserve these invaluable memories by committing them to paper, and as you enjoyed but one brief interview with Mr. Calhoun, these pages shall be addressed to you.

An eloquent member of the House of Representatives, from your State, has compared this Southern luminary to that remarkable constellation, the Southern Cross. A few years since, in sailing to a West India island, I had a perilous voyage, but have ever felt that the sight of that Southern Cross, which had long haunted my imagination, almost repaid me for its excitement and suffering. And thus do I regard an acquaintance with this intellectual star, as one great compensation for a separation from my early home. It would have been a loss not to have seen that poetic group, which greets the traveller as he sails southward, but how much greater the loss never to have beheld that unique luminary which has set to rise no more upon our visible horizon.

Mr. Calhoun's public career is so well known to you that I shall speak of him principally in his private relations, and shall refer to his opinions only as expressed in conversation—for it was in the repose of his happy home, in the tranquillity of domestic life, and in the freedom of social intercourse, that I knew him.

While the clarion-notes of his fame resound among the distant hills and valleys of our land, while those who in political strife crossed lances with this champion of the South, nobly acknowledge his valour and his honour, while Carolina chants a requiem for her departed dead, may not one who knows his moral elevation, and who has witnessed his domestic virtues, have the consolation of adding an unaffected tribute to his memory? While his devoted constituents, with impressive symbols and mournful pageants, perform funereal rites, erect for him the costly marble, weave for him the brilliant chaplet, be it mine to scatter over his honoured tomb simple but ever green leaflets. While in glowing colours the orator pourtrays him in his peerless career in the political arena, be it mine to delineate the daily beauty of his life.

In Mr. Calhoun were united the simple habits of the Spartan lawgiver, the inflexible principles of the Roman senator, the courteous bearing and indulgent kindness of the American host, husband, and father. This was indeed a rare union. Life with him was solemn and earnest, and yet all about him was cheerful. I never heard him utter a jest; there was an unvarying dignity and gravity in his manner; and yet the playful child regarded him fearlessly and lovingly. Few men indulge their families in as free, confidential, and familiar intercourse as did this great statesman. Indeed, to those who had an opportunity of observing him in his own house, it was evident that his cheerful and happy home had attractions for him superior to those which any other place could offer. Here was a retreat from the cares, the observation and the homage of the world. In few homes could the transient visitor feel more at ease than did the guest at Fort Hill. Those who knew Mr. Calhoun only by his senatorial speeches, may suppose that his heart and mind were all engaged in the nation's councils, but there were moments when his courtesy, his minute kindnesses, made you forget the statesman. The choicest fruits were selected for his guest; and I remember seeing him, at his daughter's wedding, take the ornaments from a cake and send them to a little child. Many such graceful attentions, offered in an unostentatious manner to all about him, illustrated the kindness and noble simplicity of his na-ture. His family could not but exult in his intellectual greatness, his rare endowments, and his lofty career, yet they seemed to lose sight of all these in their love for him. I had once the pleasure of travelling with his eldest son, who related to me many interesting facts and traits of his life. He said he had never heard him speak impatiently to any member of his family. He mentioned that, as he was leaving that morning for his home in Alabama, a younger brother said, "Come soon again, and see us, brother A——, for do you not see that father is growing old, and is not father the dearest, best old man in the world?"

Like Cincinnatus, he enjoyed rural life and occupation. It was his habit, when at home, to go over his grounds every day. I remember his returning one morning from a walk about his plantation, delighted with the fine specimens of corn and rice which he brought in for us to admire. That morning—the trifling incident shows his consideration and kindness of feeling, as well as his tact and power of adaptation— seeing an article of needlework in the hands of sister A——, who was then a stranger there, he examined it, spoke of the beauty of the colouring, the variety of the shade, and by thus showing an interest in her, at once made her at ease in his presence.

His eldest daughter always accompanied him to Washington, and in the absence of his wife, who was often detained by family cares at Fort Hill, this daughter was his solace amid arduous duties, and his confidant in perplexing cases. Like the gifted DeStael, she loved her father with enthusiastic devotion. Richly endowed by nature, improved by constant companionship with the great man, her mind was in harmony with his, and he took pleasure in counselling with her. She said, " Of course, I do not understand as he does, for I am comparatively a stranger to the world, yet he likes my unsophisticated opinion, and I frankly tell him my views on any subject about which he inquires of me."

Between himself and his younger daughter there was a peculiar and most tender union. As by the state of her health she was deprived of many enjoyments, her indulgent parents endeavoured to compensate for every loss by their affection and devotion. As reading was her favourite occupation, she was allowed to go to the letter-bag when it came from the office, and select the papers she preferred. On one occasion, she had taken two papers, containing news of importance, which her father was anxious to see, but he would allow no one to disturb her until she had finished their perusal.

In his social as well as in his domestic relations he was irreproachable. No shadow rested on his pure fame, no blot on his escutcheon. In his business transactions he was punctual and scrupulously exact. He was honourable as well as honest. Young men who were reared in his vicinity, with their eyes ever on him, say that in all respects, in small as well as in great things, his conduct was so exemplary that he might well be esteemed a model.

His profound love for his own family, his cordial interest in his friends, his kindness and justice in every transaction, were not small virtues in a great statesman.

He was anti-Byronic. I never heard him ridicule or satirize a human being. Indeed, he might have been thought deficient in a sense of the ludicrous, had he not, by the unvarying propriety of his own conduct, proved his exquisite perception of its opposites. When he differed in opinion from those with whom he conversed, he seemed to endeavour, by a respectful manner, to compensate for the disagreement. He employed reason rather than contradiction, and so earnestly would he urge an opinion and so fully present an argument, that his opponent could not avoid feeling complimented rather than mortified. He paid a tribute to the understandings of others by the force of his own reasoning, and by his readiness to admit every argument which he could, although advanced in opposition to one he had himself just expressed.

On one occasion I declined taking a glass of wine at his table. He kindly said, " I think you carry that a little too far. It is well to give up every thing intoxi-

cating, but not these light wines." I replied that wine
was renounced by many, for the sake of consistency,
and for the benefit of those who could not afford wine.
He acknowledged the correctness of the principle, adding, " I do not know how temperance societies can take
any other ground," and then defined his views of temperance, entered upon a course of interesting argument,
and stated facts and statistics. Of course, were all men
like Mr. Calhoun, temperance societies would be super-
fluous. Perhaps he could not be aware of the temptations which assail many men—he was so purely intellectual, so free from self-indulgence. Materiality with
him was held subject to his higher nature. He did not
even indulge himself in a cigar. Few spent as little
time and exhausted as little energy in mere amuse-
ments. Domestic and social enjoyments were his plea·
sures—kind and benevolent acts were his recreations.

He always seemed willing to converse on any subject
which was interesting to those about him. Returning
one evening from Fort Hill, I remarked to a friend, " I
have never been more convinced of Mr. Calhoun's genius than to-day, while he talked to us of a flower."
His versatile conversation evinced his universal knowledge, his quick perception, and his faculty of adaptation. A shower one day compelled him to take shelter
in the shed of a blacksmith, who was charmed by his
familiar conversation and the knowledge he exhibited
of the mechanic arts. A naval officer was once asked,
after a visit to Fort Hill, how he liked Mr. Calhoun.
"Not at all," says he—" I never like a man who knows
more about my profession than I do myself." A clergyman wished to converse with him on subjects of a
religious nature, and after the interview remarked that

he was astonished to find him better informed than himself on those very points wherein he had expected to give him information.   I have understood that Mr. Calhoun avoided an expression of opinion with regard to different sects and creeds, or what is called religious controversy; and once, when urged to give his views in relation to a disputed point, he replied, " That is a subject to which I have never given any attention."

Mr. Calhoun was unostentatious and ever averse to display.   He did not appear to talk for the sake of exhibition, but from the overflowing of his earnest nature. Whether in the Senate or in conversation with a single listener, his language was choice, his style fervid, his manner impressive.   Never can I forget his gentle earnestness when endeavouring to explain his views on some controverted subject, and observing that my mind could hardly keep pace with his rapid reasoning, he would occasionally pause and say, in his kind manner, " Do you see?"

He did not seek to know the opinions of others with regard to himself.   Anonymous letters he never read, and his daughters and nieces often snatched from the flames letters of adulation, as well as censure, which he had not read.   Although he respected the opinions of his fellow men, he did not seek office or worldly honour. A few years since, one to whom he ever spoke freely, remarked to him that some believed that he was making efforts to obtain the Presidency.   At that moment he had taken off his glasses, and was wiping them, and thus he replied :—" M——, I think when a man is too old to see clearly through his glasses, he is too old to think of the Presidency."   And recently he said to her, " They may impute what motives they please to me, but I do not seek office." So much did he respect his country, that he might have been gratified by the free gift of the people ; so much did he love his country, that he might have rejoiced at an opportunity to serve it ; but would he have swerved one iota from his convictions to secure a kingdom ? Who that knew him believes it ?

It has been said by that brilliant satirist, Horace Walpole, that every man has his price. I never did believe so evil a thing ; I have been too conversant with the great and good to believe this libel ; and I doubt not there are others beside Mr. Calhoun who value truth and honour above all price or office.

Highly as our great statesman regarded appreciation, yet he could endure to be misrepresented. While his glorious eye would light with more brilliant lustre at the greeting of friendship or the earnest expression of confidence, he rose superior to abuse or censure. I believe it was ever thus while in health. The last winter, dying in the Senate chamber, his feeble frame could ill repel the piercing shafts of his antagonists. The ebbing currents in his pulses were accelerated. He could not desert his post, though the contest raged fiercely, but his great soul was wounded. He loved his country, he loved the Union, and it was a great grief to him in his last hours to be misunderstood and misrepresented. Still, he was consoled by the thought that in the end he would be appreciated. Some one remarked to him that he was a very unpopular man. He replied, " I am, among politicians, but not among the people, and you will know this when I am dead."

Though Mr. Calhoun acknowledged, in his own winning way, the involuntary tributes of friendship and admiration, he courteously declined, whenever he could with propriety, public testimonies of homage which were offered to him.   His wife shared with him this unostentatious spirit, preferring the voice of friendship to the acclamations of the multitude.   I have heard some of his family say that they coveted nothing, not even the Presidency, for him.   They, with many of us who knew him, felt that even the first gift of a great nation could not add one gem to his crown—that crown of genius and virtue, whose glorious beauty no mortal power could illumine with new effulgence.

His sincerity was perfect.   What he thought he said. He was no diplomatist.   Some of his theories might seem paradoxical, but a paradox is not necessarily a contradiction.   He has been accused of inconsistency. Those who thus accuse him do him grievous wrong.

Nothing is more inconsistent than to persist in a uniform belief when changing circumstances demand its modification.   How absurd to preserve a law which, in the progress of society, has become null and obsolete! for instance, granting to a criminal " the benefit of clergy."   "Nothing," says a distinguished English writer, " is so revolutionary as to attempt to keep all things fixed, when, by the very laws of nature, all things are perpetually changing."   Nothing is more arrogant than for a fallible being to refuse to open his mind to conviction.   When Mr. Calhoun altered his opinion, consistency itself required the change.

However some of his political sentiments might have differed from those of many of the great and good of the age, he was sincere in them, and believed what he asserted with all the earnestness of an enthusiastic nature, with all the faith of a close and independent

thinker, and with all the confidence of one who draws
his conclusions from general principles and not from
individual facts.   Time will test the truth of his convictions.   It has been said that he was sectional in his
feelings, but surely his heart was large enough to em-
brace the whole country.   It has often been said that
he wished to dissolve the Union, but he loved the Union,
nor could he brook the thought of disunion if by any
means unity could be preserved.   Because he foresaw,
and frankly said, that certain effects must result from
certain causes, does this prove that he desired these
effects ?   In his very last speech, he speaks of disunion
as a "great disaster."   But he was not a man to cry
"peace, peace, when there was no peace."   Although
like Cassandra he might not be believed, he would raise
his warning voice; he was not a man to hide himself
when a hydra had sprung up which threatened to de-
vastate our fair and fertile land from its northern bor-
ders to its southern shores.   And while he called on
the South for union, did he not warn the conservative
party at the North that this monster was not to be
tampered with ?   And did he not call on them to unite,
and arise in their strength, and destroy it ?

And how could he, with his wise philosophy, his
knowledge of human nature, and universal benevolence,
view with indifference that unreflecting and wild (or
should I not say *savage*) philanthropy, which, in order
to sustain abstract principles, loses sight of the happiness and welfare of every class of human beings ?   How
often did he entreat that discussion on those subjects,
beyond the right of legislation, should be prevented,
that angry words and ungenerous recrimination should
cease !   Did he not foresee that such discussions would

serve to develop every element of evil in all the sections of the country—a country with such capacities for good? Did he unwisely fear that the ancient fable of Cadmus would be realized—that dragon-teeth, recklessly scattered, would spring up armed men? And did he not know that the southern heart could not remain insensible to reproach and aggression?

> " Non obtusa adeo gestamus pectora Poeni :
> Nec tam aveisus equos Tyiia Sol jungit, ab urbe."

And, ah, how earnestly did he plead for peace, and truth, and justice! As far as I understood him, he wished to benefit by his policy in affairs both the South and the North. I remember, in speaking to me of free trade, he expressed the opinion that the course he recommended would benefit the North as well as the South. This he did not merely assert, but sustained with frequent argument. In his conversation there was a remarkable blending of fact and theory, of a knowledge of the past and an insight into the future.

Mr. Calhoun was a philanthropist in the most liberal sense of the word. He desired for man the utmost happiness, the greatest good, and the highest elevation. If he differed from lovers of the race in other parts of the world, with regard to the means of obtaining these results, it was not because he failed to study the subject; not because he lacked opportunities of observation and of obtaining facts; nor because he indulged in selfish prejudices. From every quarter he gleaned accessible information, and with conscientious earnestness he brought his wonderful powers of generalization to bear on the subject of human happiness and advancement—his pure unselfish heart aiding his powerful mind.

The good of the least of God's creatures was not beneath his regard; but he did not believe that the least was equal to the greatest; he did not think the happiness or elevation of any class could be secured by a sentiment so unphilosophical. The attempt to reduce all to a level, to put all minds in uniform, to give all the same employment, he viewed as chimerical. He said that in every civilized society there must be division of labour, and he believed the slaves at the South more happy, more free from suffering and crime, than any corresponding class in any country. He had no aristocratic pride, but he desired for himself and others the highest possible elevation. He respected the artisan, the mechanic, and agriculturist, and considered each of these occupations as affording scope for native talent. He believed the African to be most happy and useful under the guidance of the Anglo-Saxon; he is averse to hard labour and responsible effort; he likes personal service, and identifies himself with those he serves.

Mr. Calhoun spoke of the great inconsistency of English denunciations of American slavery, and said that to every man, woman, and child in England, two hundred and fifty persons were tributary. Although colonial possessions and individual possessions are by many regarded as different, he considered them involved in the same general principle. In considering the rights of man, the great question is not, Has a master a right to hold a slave? but, Has one human being a right to hold another subordinate? The rights of man may be invaded, and the idol Liberty cast down, by those who are loudest in their philanthropic denunciations respecting slavery. Is there as much cruelty in holding slaves, even under the most unfavourable circumstances, as in selling into bondage a whole nation?* Let the brave chiefs of the Rohillas answer from the battle-field. Let cries from the burning cities of Rohilcund reply. Let the princesses of Oude speak from their prisons.

Close observation, prompted by a kindly heart, had brought Mr. Calhoun to the opinion that the Africans in this country were happier in existing circumstances than they would be in any other; that they were improving in their condition, and that any attempt to change it, at least at present, would not only be an evil to the country, but fraught with suffering to them. A state of freedom, so called, would be to them a state of care and disaster. To abolish slavery now would be to abolish the slave. The race would share the doom of the Indians. Although here nominally slaves, as a general thing they enjoy more freedom than any where else; for is not that freedom where one is happiest and best, and where there is a correspondence between the situation and the desires, the condition and the capacities? May we not say with the angel Abdiel

> " Unjustly thou depravest it with the name
> Of servitude, to serve whom God ordains,
> Or Nature. God and Nature bid the same,
> When he who rules is worthiest, and excels
> Them whom he governs. This is servitude,
> To serve the unwise."

Mr. Calhoun found the local attachment of the slaves so strong, their relation to their owners so satisfying to their natures, and the southern climate so congenial to them, that he did not believe any change of place or state would benefit them.

* *Vide* Macaulay's article on Warren Hastings, in the Edinburgh Review.

These, as nearly as I can recollect, were his opinions on the subject of slavery, and were expressed to me in several conversations. Sentiments similar to these are entertained by many high-minded and benevolent slaveholders. That this institution, like every other, is liable to abuse, is admitted, but every planter must answer, not for the institution—for which he is no more accountable than for the fall of Adam—but for his individual discharge of duty. If, through his selfishness, or indolenee, or false indulgence, or severity, his servants suffer, then to his Master in heaven he must give account. But those who obey the divine mandate, " Give unto your servants that which is just and equal," need not fear. In the endeavour to perform their duty in the responsible sphere in which they were placed by no act of their own, they can repose even in the midst of the wild storm which threatens devastation to our fertile lands ; they can look away from the judgment of the world, nor will they, even if all the powers of earth bid them, adopt a policy which will ruin themselves, their children, and the dependent race in their midst ; they will not cast a people they are bound to protect on the tender mercies of the cruel. In their conservative measures they are, and must be, supported at the North, by men of liberal and philosophical minds, of extended views, and benevolent hearts. But I have said far more on this subject than I intended, and will only add that those who do not, from personal observation, know this institution in its best estate, cannot easily understand the softened features it often wears, nor the high virtues exhibited by the master, and the confiding, dependent attachment of the servant. Often is the Southern planter as a patriarch in olden times. Those who are striving to sever his household know not what they do.

Well may we who live in these troubled times exclaim, with Madame Roland, the martyr of the false principles of her murderers, "O Liberte! O Liberte! que de crimes on commet en ton nom!" This she said, turning to the statue of Liberty beside the scaffold. Liberty unrestrained degenerates into license. There may be political freedom without social liberty. Says Lamartine, speaking of the inhabitants of Malta, "Ils sont esclaves de la loi immuable de la force que Dieu leur fait; nous sommes esclaves des lois variables et capricieuses que nous nous faisons."

A few years' residence on this soil might teach even a Wilberforce to turn in his philanthropy to other and wider fields of action.

Of Mr. Calhoun's character as a master, much might be said, for all who knew him admit that it was exemplary. But we need not multiply examples to prove his unaffected goodness, and I will repeat only a circumstance or two, which, by way of illustrating some subjects discussed, he incidentally mentioned to me. One relating to a free negro, formerly a slave in Carolina, but then living in one of our Northern cities, who came to him in Washington, begging him to intercede for his return to Carolina. He represented his condition as deplorable, said that he could not support himself and family by his trade, (he was a shoemaker,) and that not being able to obtain sufficient food and fuel in that cold climate, they were almost frozen. " When I told him," said Mr. Calhoun, "that I would do all I could for him, he seized both my hands in his, and expressed fervent gratitude." At another time, speaking of a family whom his son designed to take to Alabama, he told me that the mother of the family came to him and said she would prefer to stay with her master and mistress on the plantation, even if all her children went with master A. Mr. Calhoun added, " I could not think of her remaining without either of her children; and as she chose to stay, we retained her youngest son, a boy of twelve years."

Mr. Calhoun required very little of any one, doing more for others than he asked of them. He seemed to act upon the principle that the strong should bear the burthens of the weak. In sickness he feared to give trouble, and, unless his friends insisted, would have little done for him. " Energetic as he was," said a near relative, " he would lie patiently all day, asking for nothing." His sensibility was of the most unselfish nature. Some months before his death, and after he left Fort Hill the last time, he said he felt that death was near, much nearer than he was willing to have his family know, and added that he wished to give all the time he could spare from public duty to preparation for death. While suffering from increasing illness at Washington, still, as he hoped to return again to his family, he was unwilling, though they anxiously awaited his summons, that they should be alarmed, saying he could not bear to see their grief. No doubt his conscientious spirit felt that his country, at that critical moment, demanded his best energies, and that he should be unnerved by the presence of his nearest friends; and loving his own family as he did, and beloved as he was by them, he serenely awaited the approach of the King of Terrors, and suffered his last sorrow far from his home, cheered only by one watcher from his household.

There was a beautiful adaptation in his bearing—a just appreciation of what was due to others, and a nice sense of propriety. I have had opportunities to compare his manners with those of other great men. His kind and unaffected interest was expressed in a way peculiarly dignified and refined. Some men appear to think they atone for a low estimate of our sex by flattery. Not so with Mr. Calhoun. He paid the highest compliment which could be paid to woman, by recognizing in her a soul—a soul capable of understanding and appreciating. Of his desire for her improvemnt and elevation he gave substantial proofs. Although Fort Hill was five miles from the Female Academy, he never suffered an examination to pass without honouring it with his presence. He came not for the sake of form, but he exhibited an interest in the exercises, and was heard to comment upon them afterwards in a manner which showed that he had given them attention. He never reminded you that his hours were more precious than yours. The question may be asked how could he, amid his great and stern duties, find time for attention to those things from which so many men excuse themselves on the plea of business. But he wasted no time, and by gathering up its fragments, he had enough and to spare. I have before said that his kind acts were his recreations.

Were I asked wherein lay the charm which won the hearts of all who came within his circle, I could not at once reply. It was, perhaps, his perfect *abandon*, his sincerity, his confidential manner, his childlike simplicity, in union with his majestic intelligence, and his self-renunciation—the crowing virtue of his life ; these imparted the vivid enjoyment and the delightful repose which his friends felt in his presence.   It was often not so much what he said, as his manner of saying it, that was so impressive.   Never can I forget an incident which occurred at the time when a war with England, on account of Oregon, seemed impending.   He arrived in Charleston during the excitement on that subject. He was asked in the drawing-room if he thought there would be a war.   He waived an answer, saying that for some time he had been absent from home and had received no official documents; but as he passed with us from the drawing-room to the street door, he said to me, in his rapid, earnest manner, " I anticipate a severe seven months' campaign.   I have never known our country in such a state."   War has a terror for me, and I said, " Oh, Mr. Calhoun, do not let a war arise. Do all you can to prevent it."   He replied, " I will do all, in honour, I can do," and paused.   A thousand thoughts seemed to pass over his face, his soul was in his eyes, and bending a little forward, as if bowed by a sense of his responsibility and insufficiency, he added, speaking slowly and with emphasis, and with the deepest solemnity, as if questioning with himself, " *But what can one man do ?*"   I see him now.   No painting or sculpture could remind me so truly of him as does my faithful memory.   But I will not dwell on the subject, for I fear I can never, by words, convey to the mind of another the impression which I received of his sincerity, and of his devotion to his country and to the cause of humanity.   How he redeemed his pledge to do all that he, in honour, could do, his efforts in the settlement of the Oregon question truly show.   When next I saw him I told him how much I was delighted with his Oregon speech.   In his kindest manner he replied, "I am glad I can say any thing to please you."

The last time I saw Mr. Calhoun, you, my brother, were with me. You remember that his kind wife took us to his room, and that you remarked the cheerfulness and affability with which he received us, although his feeble health had obliged him to refuse almost every one that day. We shall see him no more, but his memory will linger with us.

To you I would commend him as an example. Read his letter to a young lawyer. As you are so soon to enter the profession of law, such a model as Mr. Calhoun may be studied with advantage. While I would never wish one to lose his own individuality, or to descend to imitation, I believe that one gifted mind leaves its impress on another; while I would not deify or canonize a mortal, I would render homage to one who united such moral attainments to so rare a combination of intellectual gifts; while it is degrading to ourselves and injurious to others to lavish unmerited and extravagant praise, it is a loss not to appreciate a character like his, for it ennobles our own nature to contemplate the true and the beautiful.

Although it is said that our country is in danger from its ideas of equality, and its want of reverence and esteem for age, and wisdom, and office, and talents, and attainments, and virtues—and this feature of the American character is so strongly impressed, that Mar Yohannah, the Nestorian bishop, said in my presence, in his peculiar English, " Yes, I know this nation glory in its republicanism, but I am afraid it will become republican to God"—yet it is a cheering omen when a man like Mr. Calhoun is so much beloved and reverenced. I think every one who was favoured with a personal acquaintance with him, will admit that I have not been guilty of exaggeration, and "will delight to do him honour."

The question naturally arises, to what are we to ascribe the formation of such a character? There must have been causes for such effects. Whence came his temperance, his self-denial, his incorruptible integrity, his fidelity in every duty, his love for mankind, his indefatigable efforts for the good of others, and his superiority to those things which the natural heart most craves? Mr. Calhoun's childhood was spent among the glorious works of nature, and was sheltered from the temptations which abound in promiscuous society. He was the son of pious parents, and by them he was taught the Bible, and from that source undoubtedly his native gifts were perfected. I have understood that from early life he was an advocate for the doctrines of the Bible, as understood by orthodox Christians. I have been told by relatives of his, who were on the most intimate terms with him, that for some time before his death his mind had seemed to be much occupied with religious subjects, and that he too often expressed confidence in the providence of God, to leave any doubt as to his trust in Him. An eminent clergyman, now deceased, said in conversation with another, that he had often conversed with Mr. Calhoun on the subject of religion, and had no doubt as to his piety. I have remarked his reverential air in church, and have known him apparently much disturbed by any inattention in others. He never united with any church; and it is my opinion, formed not without some reason, that he was prevented, not by disregard to any Christian ordinances, but from personal and conscientious scruples with respect to his qualifications. He was a man who weighed everything with mathematical precision.

Although open as day on topics of general interest, he was reserved in respect to himself. I do not recollect ever to have heard him speak egotistically, for his mind seemed always engrossed by some great thought; and he appears, even at the close of life, to lose all personal solicitudes in his anxiety for his country. In one of his last letters he says, " But I must close. This may be my last communication to you. My end is probably near—perhaps very near. Before I reach it I have but one serious thought to gratify—it is to see my country quieted under some arrangement (alas, I know not what!) that will be satisfactory to all, and safe to the South." His country's peace, and quietness, and safety, he did not see ; he perished in the storm ; and there are many who knew and loved him, who cherish the hope that he is removed to a higher sphere of action—that his noble spirit has meekly entered into the presence of its author; and that, in the starry courts above, he will receive an inheritance " incorruptible, undefiled, and that fadeth not away."

When I saw the elaborate preparations which were made here in Charleston for his funeral, knowing his simple tastes and habits, and his benevolence, I was at first pained, and I thought he would not have sanctioned so much display. I feared, too, that solemnity would be lost in pageantry. But it was not so. There was nothing to jar upon the feelings of the most sensitive. All was in perfect and mournful harmony. Silently and reverently his sorrowing countrymen bore his remains from the steamer where they had reposed under a canopy wearing its thirty stars, and when the hearse, so funereal with mournful drapery and sable plumes, entered the grounds of the Citadel, deep silence brooded over the vast multitude ; noiselessly were heads uncovered, banners dropped—not a sound but that of the tramp of horses was heard ; statue-like was that phalanx, with every eye uplifted to the sacred sarcophagus. If there was too much of show, it was redeemed by the spirit that prompted it : the symbols, significant and expressive as they were, faintly shadowed forth the deep and universal grief ; the mournful pageantry, the tolling bell, the muffled drum, the closed and shrouded stores and houses, gave external signs of woe ; but more impressive and affecting was the peaceful sadness which brooded over the metropolis while it awaited the relics of the patriot, and the deep silence which pervaded the vast procession that followed to the City Hall—the subdued bearing of the crowd who resorted thither, and the solemnity expressed on every face ; for these told that the great heart of the city and the commonwealth wept in hushed and sincere sorrow over " the mighty fallen in the midst of the battle."

One day and night the illustrious dead reposed in state in the draped and darkened hall. An entrance was formed by the arching Palmetto, that classic tree, under whose branches Dudon, the Crusader, was placed, when slain in Palestine. On that tree—" altissima palma"—his comrades placed his trophies. With a spirit as sad as that of the Crusaders when under the verdant foliage of the palm they mourned the noble Dudon, did those who loved our champion pass be-

neath that arch, dark with funereal gloom. The sarcophagus was within a magnificent catafalque; the
canopy rested on Corinthian columns; the bier was
apparently supported by six urns, while three pale-
coloured eagles surmounted the canopy, holding in their
beaks the waving crape. Invisible lamps cast moon-
light beams over the radiated upper surface of the
canopy. Through the day numbers resorted to this
hallowed spot, and at night vigils were held where the
dead reposed. When the morning came, the chosen
guards carried the remains of the great leader to the
church. The funeral car was not allowed to bear these
sacred relics to the tomb, but they were borne by
sons of the State, with uncovered heads. Well might
those who saw their self-forgetfulness, their devotion
to the memory of this great and good statesman, feel
that Carolina would never be wanting to herself. They
placed him upon the bier, surrounded by significant
offerings—pure flowers and laurel-wreaths. A velvet
pall, revealing in silver lines the arms of the State, the
Palmetto, covered the sarcophagus. Above it was a
coronet woven of laurel leaves, like that which crown-
ed Tasso. Then in that church, where mournfully
waved the sable crape, where columns, arches, and
galleries were shrouded in the drapery of woe—symbols of the sorrowing hearts gathered there—the funeral rites were performed. Then was the mighty dead
placed in his narrow tomb. Over it the choicest
flowers were scattered; above it waved the nation's
flag.

Weep, Columbia, for a philanthropist, an American
patriot, has fallen! Lament, sons and daughters of
Carolian—"hang your harps upon the willows," for

" your Washington" has fallen. Revive the Roman heroic honours, for a greater than a Roman lies here :

> " Manibus date lilia plenis,
> Purpureos spargam flores."

Peerless statesman, illustrious counsellor, devoted patriot, generous friend, indulgent husband and father, thy humble, noble heart is still in death ; thy life was yielded up at the post of duty ; thou hast perished like a sentinel on guard—a watchman in his tower. " Thou wast slain in thy high places." Clouds gathered thick and fast about thy country's horizon, and even thy eagle eye failed in its mournful gaze to penetrate the gloom which hides its future from mortal eye. Thy work is finished—peacefully rest with thine own ! Thy memory is enshrined in the hearts of those for whom thy heart ceased its beating. Thy grave is with us—

> " Yet spirit immortal, the tomb cannot bind thee,
>   For like thine own eagle eye that soared to the sun,
> Thou springest from bondage, and leavest behind thee
>   A name which before thee few mortals have won."

In reviewing the character of Mr. Calhoun, we find a rare combination of mental and moral qualities—a union of contrasts. He combined genius with common sense, the power of generalization with the habit of abstraction, rapidity of thought with application and industry. His mind was suggestive and logical, imaginative and practical. His noble ideal was embodied in his daily life. He was at once discursive and profound ; he could soar like the eagle, or hover on unwearied wings around a minute circle. He meekly bore his lofty endowments ; his childlike simplicity imparted a charm to his transcendent intellect ; he united dignity with humility, sincerity with courtesy, decision with gentleness, stern inflexibility with winning urbanity, and keen sensibility with perfect self-command. He was indulgent to others, denying to himself; he was energetic in health, and patient in sickness; he combined strict temperance with social habits; he was reserved in communicating his personal feelings, but his heart was open on subjects of general interest; he prized the regard of his fellow-beings, but was superior to worldly pomps and flatteries; he honoured his peers, but was not swayed by their opinions. Equal to the greatest, he did not despise the least of men. He did not neglect one duty to perform another. In the Senate he was altogether a senator; in private and domestic life he was as though he had never entered the halls of the nation, and had never borne an illustrious part in the councils of his country.